Trombone Student

by Paul Tanner and Major Herman Vincent
in collaboration with James Ployhar

To the Student

Level III of the Belwin "Student Instrumental Course" is a continuation of Levels I and II of this series or may be used to follow any other good intermediate instruction book. It is designed to help you become an excellent player on your instrument in a most enjoyable manner. It will take a reasonable amount of work and CAREFUL practice on your part. If you do this, learning to play should be a valuable and pleasant experience.

Please see the top of Page 3 for practice suggestions and other comments that should be very helpful.

To the Teacher

Level III of this series is a continuation of the Belwin "Student Instrumental Course", which is the first and only complete course for individual instruction of all band instruments. Like instruments may be taught in classes. Cornets, Trombones, Baritones and Basses may be taught together. The course is designed to give the student a sound musical background and, at the same time, provide for the highest degree of interest and motivation. The entire course is correlated to the band oriented sequence.

Each page of this book is planned as a complete lesson, however, because some students advance more rapidly than others, and because other lesson situations may vary, lesson assignments are left to the discretion of the teacher.

To make the course both authoritative and practical, the books in Level III are co-authored by a national authority on each instrument in collaboration with James Ployhar.

The Belwin "Student Instrumental Course" has three levels: elementary, intermediate and advanced intermediate. Each level consists of a method and two or three supplementary books. Levels II and III each have four separate correlated solos with piano accompaniment. The chart below shows the correlating books available with each part.

The Belwin "STUDENT INSTRUMENTAL COURSE" - A course for individual and class instruction of LIKE instruments, at three levels, for all band instruments.

EACH BOOK IS COMPLETE IN ITSELF BUT ALL BOOKS ARE CORRELATED WITH EACH OTHER

METHOD
"The Trombone Student"
For Individual
or
Brass Class Instruction.

ALTHOUGH EACH BOOK CAN BE USED SEPARATELY, IDEALLY, ALL SUPPLEMENTARY BOOKS SHOULD BE USED AS COMPANION BOOKS WITH THE METHOD

STUDIES AND MELODIOUS ETUDES

Supplementary scales, warm-up and technical drills, musicianship studies and melody-like etudes, all carefully correlated with the method.

TUNES FOR TECHNIC

Technical type melodies, variations, and "famous passages" from musical literature for the development of technical dexterity.

TROMBONE SOLOS

Four separate correlated solos, with piano accompaniment, written or arranged by Paul Tanner:
I Ain't Gonna Study War No More . . . . *Anonymous*
Nine Hundred Miles . . . . *Anonymous*
The Clarion . . . . *Tanner*
Dawn is the Beginning . . . *Tanner*

CORRELATED TROMBONE SOLOS

Four separate solos, with piano accompaniment, were written or arranged specifically for this course. We strongly encourage the use of these solos as supplementary lesson material.

I Ain't Gonna Study War No More
. . . . *arranged by Paul Tanner*

Nine Hundred Miles
. . . . *arranged by Paul Tanner*

The Clarion . . . . *Paul Tanner*

Dawn Is The Beginning . . . . *Paul Tanner*

SLIDE POSITION CHART

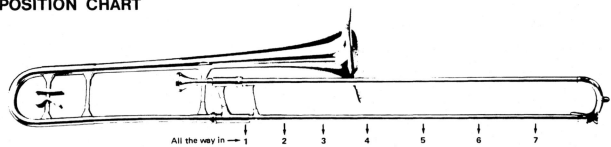

All the way in → 1   2   3   4   5   6   7

When two notes are shown together on the chart (F♯ and G♭), they have the same sound and are played on the same position.

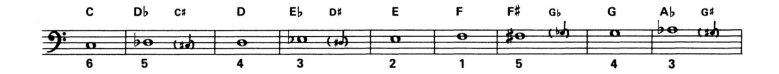

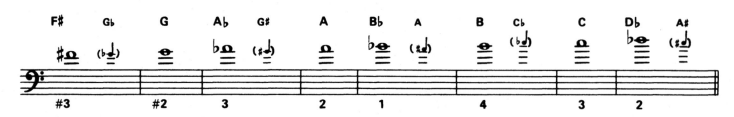

Position marked with a sharp are just a little shorter than normal, listen for correct intonation at all times.

A Few Important Practice Suggestions

1. Set a regular practice time and make every effort to practice at this time.

2. ALWAYS practice carefully. Careless practice is a waste of time. Learn to play each line exactly as written. Later there may be times when certain freedoms may be taken.

3. The instrument must always be clean and in good playing condition.

4. The development of careful and accurate playing habits is essential if you are to become a good player. Proper hand, finger, mouth or embouchure, and body position is absolutely necessary for best results. Always keep relaxed.

5. COUNT AT ALL TIMES.

Remember — Music should be fun but the better player you are the more
fun you have. It takes work to become a good player.

Daily Warm-Up Studies

The lines below are intended for use as daily warm-up drill, embouchure or lip-building studies, and for the development of technical proficiency. They should be used as an addition or supplement to the regular lesson assignment.

Use certain lines as a daily routine with changes from time to time as suggested by your teacher.

B.I.C.356

Lip Slurs

Scale Study In B♭

Chromatics

ARTICULATION

Staccato Slur Accents Tenuto Sforzando *(with sudden emphasis)*

March Melody

March tempo

Please see the book "Tunes for Trombone Technic", level III, for more melodies that provide for further technical development.

G Minor *(Harmonic Form)*   Arpeggios

G Minor *(Melodic Form)*   Arpeggios

Etude In G Minor

A Comparison Study In G Major

ARPEGGIO ETUDE

Slowly

To The Waltz

TSCHAIKOWSKY

Vivace

B.I.C.356

5

INTERVALS

Practice slowly, then try for speed, giving special emphasis on the accented notes.

Articulation Etude

KOPPRASCH

Allegro

Dutch Air

A PHRASING STUDY

Work for speed

RHYTHM ETUDE

Compare measures 1 & 3. Play accurately.

The Wild Horseman

SCHUMANN

Allegro

D.C. al Fine

Special Page For Trombone Only
Slide Movement

All trombone instruction insists that the player have the slide in the exact correct spot at the time that the note is tongued. As a consequence, there is a considerable tendency to actually stop the slide action as each note is played, this gives a feeling of security regarding intonation. Intonation is surely one of the most important elements of music; however, stopping the slide for every note in a fairly rapid passage will certainly be a great hinderance to fast technique. It is possible, with great concentration, and even greater listening, to keep the slide moving as long as it is going in one direction, professional trombonists find this very important. While playing the following passages, listen to the pitch of each note, watch the slide and make sure that as you tongue each note, that the slide is where it should be, but keep it moving while playing these short notes.

LIP SLURS

① Slowly

6th position ___ *5* ___ *4* ___

Scale Study In E♭ Major

②

Syncopation Study

③

Count: 1 & 2 & 3 & 4 & 1 & 2 & 3 & 4 & etc.

Interval Study

④

Theme From Rigoletto

VERDI

⑤ Allegretto

f *leggiero [light and graceful]*

rit. *a tempo*

cresc. *rit.* *a tempo*

INTERVALS

Play accurately and "lean" on the top note.

Articulation Etude

Slowly — steady, then gradaully faster.

Comparing 𝅘𝅥𝅮𝅘𝅥𝅮 And 𝅘𝅥𝅮𝅘𝅥𝅮.

Benny Havens

Andante

Etude

ARBAN

Moderato

Lip Slurs

6th position _____ 5 _____ 4 _____

Fingering Exercise In F

Play at your own tempo, but steady.

Syncopation Study

(In two)

Waltz Melody

A TONE & PHRASING STUDY

BRAHMS

p dolce [smoothly]

Etude

SMALL

Moderato

mf

a tempo

rall.   dim.

D Minor *(Harmonic Form)*   **Arpeggios**

D Minor *(Melodic Form)*   **Arpeggios**

D Minor Scale Study (Melodic Form)

Grace Notes

As written:

Grace notes are small eighth notes with a dash through the stem. It precedes the beat and is played fast, light and unaccented. See page 39.

As played:

Song Of The Mermaids

WEBER

Andante con moto

p   dolce

rall.

Lip Slurs

Articulation Study

ARBAN

ABBREVIATIONS

Rhythm Etude

Artist's Life

J. STRAUSS

OCTAVE SLURS

Scale Study In A♭

Slow, accurate, then try for speed.

Interval Study

Grace Notes*

As written:

As played:

Theme From Rigoletto

VERDI

*
See page 39.

F Minor (Harmonic Form)

F Minor (Melodic Form)

①

Arpeggios

②

Also 8va (play octave lower)

Study In F Minor

③

Syncopation Study

④

Count: 1 & 2 & 3 &   1 & 2 & 3 &   etc.

CHROMATICS

⑤

Polonaise Militaire

CHOPIN

Allegro con brio

⑥

*see note
[8va opt.] -

Fine

D.C. al Fine

Note: Three evenly divided sixteenth notes (triplets) may be played in place of an eighth note.

B.I.C.356

Intervals

"Hear" the pitch before you play.

High Register

RHYTHM STUDY

Articulation

Allegro vivace

Grace Note Etude

Andante

D.C. al Coda

Coda

rall.

LIP SLURS

Scale Study In C

Tonguing Exercise

ARBAN

A Reading Exercise

Andante From A Major Symphony

MENDELSSOHN

INTERVALS

Grace Notes

Moderato (♩ = 60)

LAURENT

LOW REGISTER STUDY

Work for speed!

Since a dot placed after a note adds one-half of its value, two dots placed after a note will add one-half plus one-quarter of its value.

As written:

As played:

March Pontificale

C. GOUNOD

Allegro

LIP SLURS

① 4th position

② 5th position

Articulation Study

LAURENT

③ Andante

p leggiero

f

p

OCTAVE SLURS

④ Slowly

Comparing 6/8 And 12/8

⑤ Count: 1 2 1 2 etc.

Count: 1 2 3 4 etc.

Andante Cantabile

TSCHAIKOWSKY

⑥ Slowly

mf

Accuracy

Lento

Remove the instrument from the mouth, and re-position embouchure for each note.

Rhythm And Articulation Etude

Allegro (♩ = 80)

Play with precise rhythm.

Scale Study In D♭ Major

Etude

SMALL

Waltz tempo

Coda

rall.

D.C. al ⊕

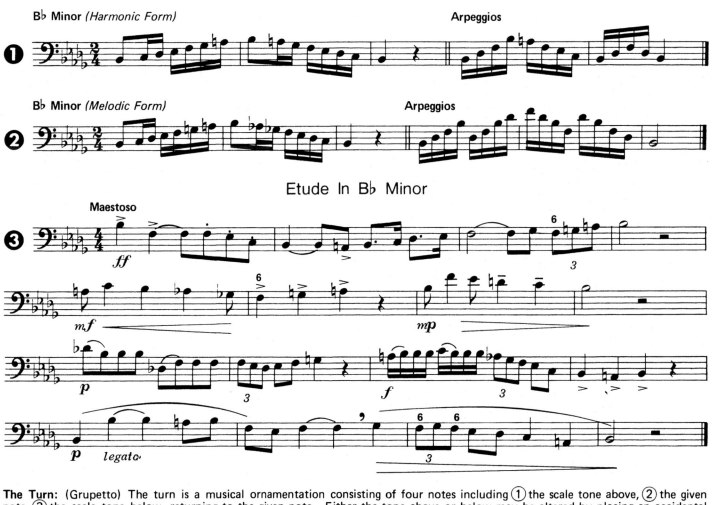

The Turn: (Grupetto) The turn is a musical ornamentation consisting of four notes including ① the scale tone above, ② the given note, ③ the scale tone below, returning to the given note. Either the tone above or below may be altered by placing an accidental above or below the sign which is ∾ (See page 40.)

Intervals

Articulation

Rhythm Study

Etude

① **E Minor** *(Harmonic Form)*   **Arpeggios**

② **E Minor** *(Melodic Form)*   **Arpeggios**

Etude In E Minor

③ **Allegro**

Tonguing Study

④ **Allegro moderato**   SMALL

mf

rit.

a tempo

p dolce

A La Nanita Nana

A PHRASING STUDY   TRADITIONAL
Larghetto   SPANISH CAROL

⑤ *p*

legato e dolce   *dim.*   *Fine*

mf   *p*

a tempo

mp   *p*   *rit.*   *D.C. al Fine*

INTERVALS

Etude In G Major

The Trill

The trill is a rapid alternation of a given note and the note above (in the diatonic scale). It may be either a half or whole step. If an accidental is placed with the trill, it alters the upper note. (See page 40)

Trill Study

Andante

dolce

Phrasing Study

Moderato

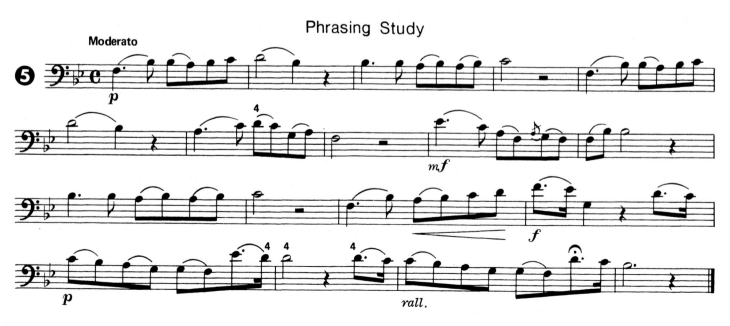

Special Page For Trombone Only
Lip Trills

The trill is a peculiar problem for the slide trombone. Composers and conductors expect the trill note to be the next tone above the given note in the diatonic scale. This premise works well for instruments with valves; but for slide, this is sometimes an actual physical impossibility. Therefore, professional trombonists rely on the lip trill. This means that there is rapid alternation between the given note and the next natural overtone above. The problem is that the interval between the given note and the trill note varies according to where the given note is on the overtone series. When a Bb is trilled, the interval is a major 3rd (Ex.1); when a D above the staff is trilled, the interval is a minor 3rd (Ex.2); the G above that is trilled with an A, a whole step above (Ex.3).

The practice of the trill also aids flexibility.   Use no tongue at all.

Gb Major Scale ... **Arpeggios**

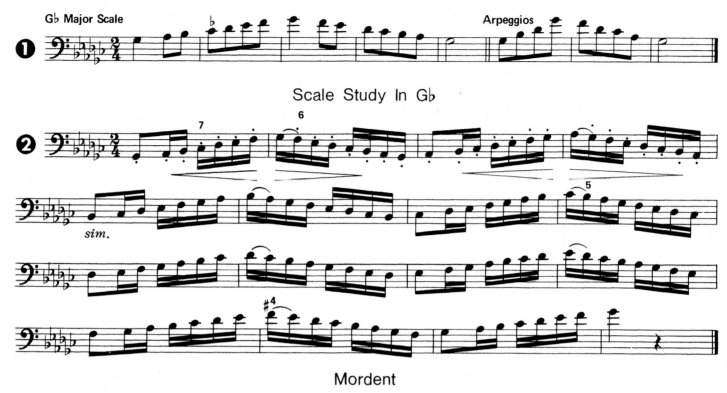

Scale Study In Gb

sim.

Mordent

The Mordent is an ornamentation or embellishment of the rapid alternation of a given note with the note immediately below in the scale. ᨘ The inverted mordent alternates the given note with the note above. ᨘ (See page 39)

As written: As played: As written: As played:

Inverted Mordent

Minuet

ST. JACOME

Presto (in one)

March From Nutcracker Suite

TSCHAIKOWSKY

March moderato

mf

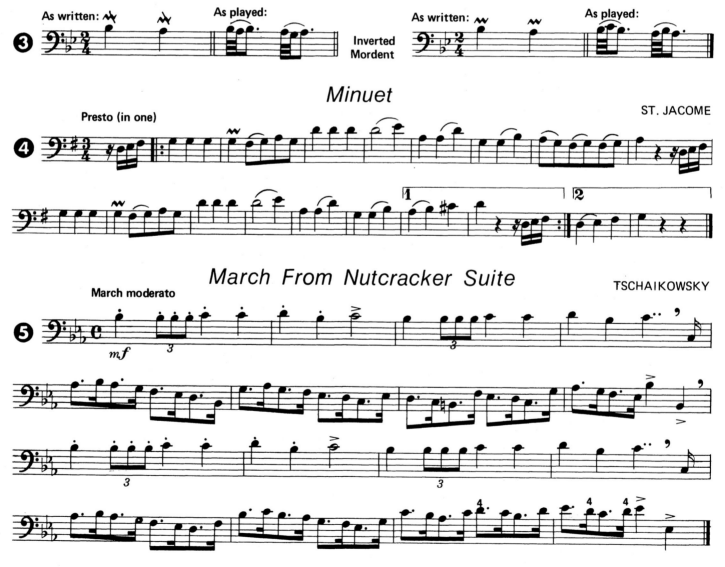

Lip Slurs

Articulation Study

Chromatics

HIGH RANGE STUDY

Theme From La Traviata

VERDI

Allegro brilliante

Eb Minor *(Harmonic Form)*   Arpeggios

Eb Minor *(Melodic Form)*   Arpeggios

Interval Study

Articulation Study

Etude In Eb Minor

(♩ = 120)

Flexibility Study

Chromatics

Tonguing Endurance

LAURENT

Start in 4/4 ; then fast to ¢.

f *leggiero*

sim.

Etude

Tempo ad lib.

mf

Waltz

CHOPIN

Vivo (original key — E♭)

f

D Major Scale

Arpeggios

①

Scale Study In D Major

Work for speed!

②

INTERVAL SLURS

③

Study In Eb Minor

④

Theme From "Washington Grays" March

GRAFULLA

⑤

p

f

B.I.C.356

30

Lip Slurs

INTERVALS

Triple Tonguing

Triple tonguing is a technique of executing fast triplet passages utilizing the syllables Tu Tu Ku, or Ta Ta Ka. Before applying them to the Trombone, practice them verbally.

Tu Tu Ku Tu Tu Ku Tu Tu Ku Tu Tu Ku   Tu

ARBAN

Slowly — then increase speed.

Tu Tu Ku Tu Tu Ku Tu

Tu Tu Ku Tu Tu Ku Tu Tu Ku Tu

A Phrasing Study

Andante

Additional Triple and Double Tonguing Exercises may be found in "Studies and Melodious Etudes", Level III.

Arpeggios

Reading Flexibility

Double Tonguing

The performing of fast duplet passages requires a technique known as double tonguing. This is achieved by the use of the syllables Tu-Ku repeated in rapid succession. First practice them verbally before applying to the trombone.

ARBAN

Tu Ku Tu Ku Tu   *sim.*

Relax

mf p mf

3 $cresc.$ f p $rit.$

Additional Triple and Double Tonguing Exercises may be found in "Studies and Melodious Etudes", Level III.

Chromatic Study

The Cadenza is a free, improvisatory section of a composition usually utilized near the end of the piece. It is designed to give the player a welcome chance to exhibit his technical brilliance. There is no set tempo, however extreme accelerando and ritard usually lead to each formata.

Theme From La Traviata

VERDI

Lip Slurs

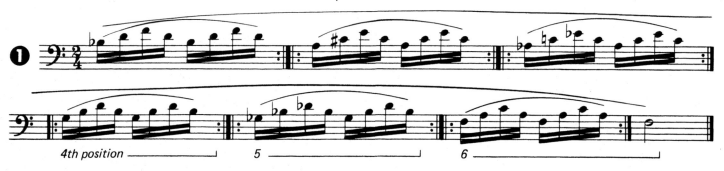

Repeat each measure several times. When all are smooth, play entire exercise without repeats.

Scales

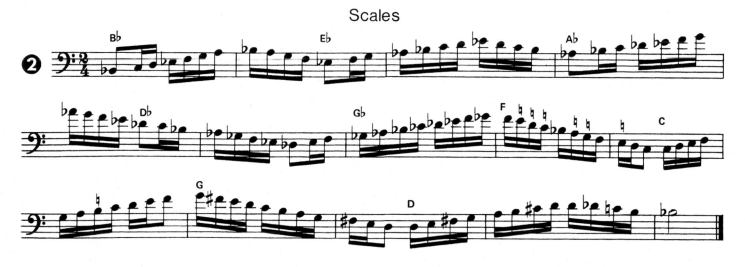

Articulation

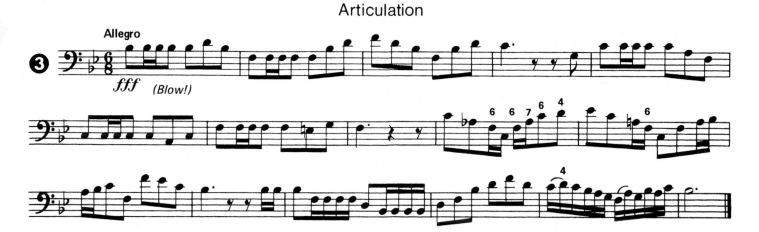

A Study In Rhythm

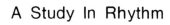

5 Trombone — Tacet

Special Page For Trombone Only

Tenor And Alto Clefs

In orchestral playing, you may be asked to play your part in some clef other than bass clef, this would be tenor clef or alto clef. As the bass clef is sometimes called an F clef because the two dots enclose F, the tenor and alto clefs are sometimes called C clefs because they specifically designate where middle C is located:

The most used of these two C clefs is the tenor clef, but older orchestral literature often uses alto clef for the first trombone parts.

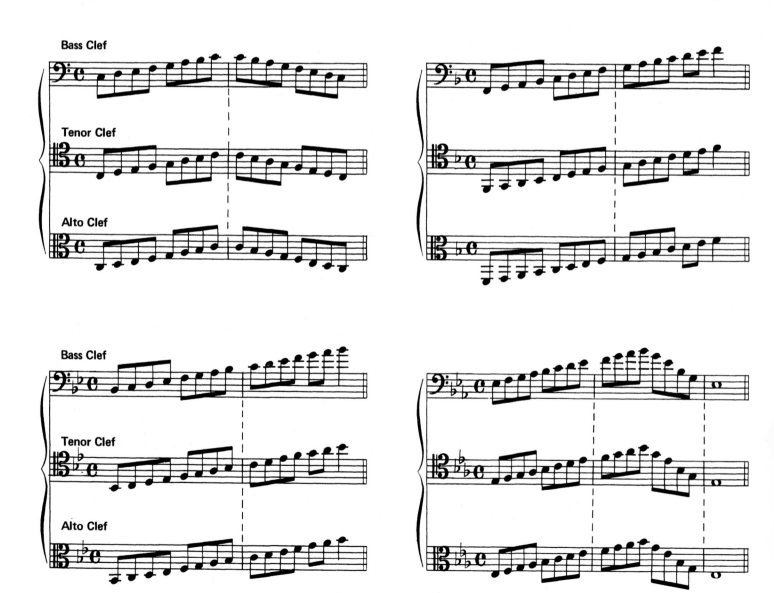

Characteristic Studies*

*STUDIES AND MELODIOUS ETUDES, Level III, deals with these last rather difficult passages. It is strongly recommended that you refer to it as a supplement to the Method.

B.I.C.356

Basic Technic
Lip Slurs

Chromatic Scales

Articulations

Apply to above:

Intervals

Allegro

Basic Technic (cont'd)
Triple Tonguing

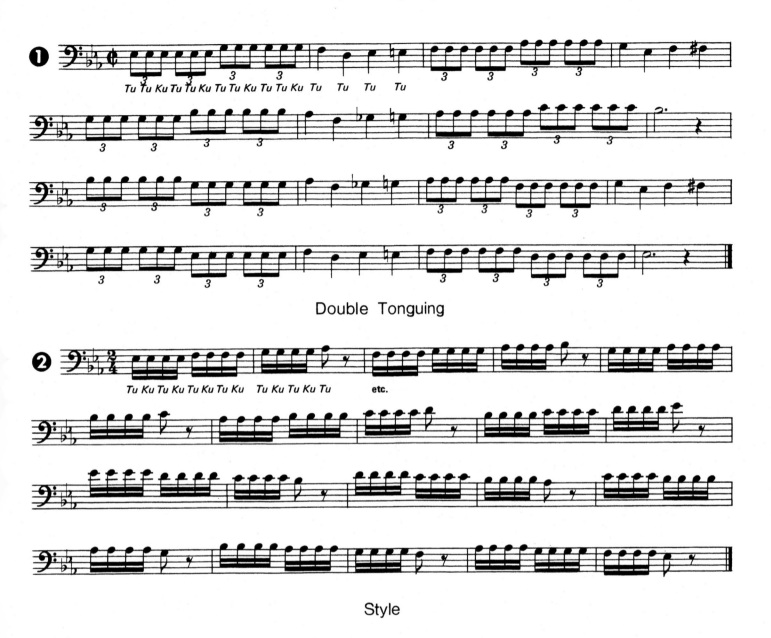

Tu Tu Ku Tu Tu Ku Tu Tu Ku Tu Tu Ku Tu   Tu   Tu   Tu

Double Tonguing

Tu Ku Tu Ku Tu Ku Tu Ku   Tu Ku Tu Ku Tu   etc.

Style

It should be brought to mind at this time that we have tried to present you with the material, instruction and the supplementary books necessary for developing the mechanical aspects of playing the trombone. With these tools, you the player must now become a musician and develop your own style of performance. Always remember, DON'T PLAY NOTES, PLAY MUSIC!!!

March (Sousa)
Classical (Handel) Maestoso
Opera (Verdi) lyrically Andante

Special Page For Trombone Only

VIBRATO

The most controversial embellishment for sound on the trombone is vibrato. There are great differences of opinion as to when to use vibrato, some instruction even avoids mentioning this embellishment at all. However, all professional trombonists do use vibrato at sometime in the music they perform. Listen very intently to develop discernment regarding when to use vibrato and when not to use it.

There are two standard means of applying vibrato on the slide trombone. One is by a very slight movement of the lower lip while sustaining a tone. Make sure that this movement is very minimal, and also make sure that you can start and stop this movement at any desired instant. The other method is by moving the slide quickly just a little above and below the desired pitch. Vibrato is seldom used below D in the staff; and in this lower pitch area, the vibrato is usually slower and more narrow than in the upper register.

In order to practice the use of vibrato, merely start a tone, make sure you have the exact pitch you want with the best possible tone, then add the vibrato. With the vibrato now added, make doubly sure that the pure tone itself has not suffered and that the intonation has remained exactly where you want it, do not let the vibrato cause faulty intonation. Make sure that the vibrato does not "take over" the sound, it is merely an embellishment just as in the male voice in that same register, it helps the flow of certain musical passages.

B.I.C.356

MUSICAL EMBELLISHMENTS
Grace Notes

A SHORT grace note is written as a small eighth note with a dash through its stem.   The grace note precedes the beat and is played in a light unaccented manner.

The SHORT grace note may appear as single, double, triple or quadruple notation.   However, they should still be played ahead of the beat on which the principal note appears.

The LONG grace note (appoggiatura) does not have a dash through its stem and is played on the beat.   The long grace note is assigned half the time value of the principal note.   However, if it precedes a dotted note, the grace note would receive two-thirds the time value of the principal note.

The Mordent

The MORDENT is a musical ornamentation consisting of a rapid alternation of the given note with the note immediately below it in the scale.   The sign for the mordent is ♵.   The INVERTED MORDENT consists of the alternation of the given note and the note immediately above in the scale.   The sign for the inverted mordent is ∿.

The Trill

The TRILL is a musical ornamentation consisting of the rapid alternation of a given note and the next note above in the diatonic scale. The interval may be a whole step or a half step. If an accidental accompanies the trill sign it alters the upper tone.

Longer trills are closed by playing a note on scale step below the given note, followed by the given note.

For solo playing it is advisable to start the trill slowly and gradually increase the speed.

The Turn (Gruppetto)

The TURN is a musical ornamentation consisting of four notes including 1 the scale tone above the given note, 2 the given note, 3 the scale tone below the given note, and 4 the given note again. The turn is indicated by this sign ∾. The turn is executed very rapidly near the end of the duration of the given note.

When a turn is to be executed after a dotted note, the last note of the turn is given the same value as the dot (Ex.1). If an accidental is placed under a turn, it alters the lower note (Ex.2). If an accidental is placed over a turn, it alters the upper note (Ex.3). If the turn is placed DIRECTLY over the given note, it is executed very rapidly starting on the tone above the given note (Ex.4)